SEA LIFE MANDALAS
COLORING BOOK

JO TAYLOR

DOVER PUBLICATIONS, INC.
MINEOLA, NEW YORK

These 63 striking mandala images, specially designed for advanced colorists, will appeal to those who enjoy the symbolism of these unique circular designs as well as those who enjoy the allure of sea life and nature. This deluxe edition features a diverse array of sea creatures that range from the familiar to the exotic. Here you will find Hawaiian sea turtles, coral fish, sea anemones, angelfish, pelicans, raccoon butterflyfish, leopard stingrays, and much more— all artistically rendered in the mesmerizing symmetry of mandala patterns. Plus, the pages are perforated and printed on one side only for easy removal and display.

Copyright

Copyright © 2017 by Dover Publications, Inc.
All rights reserved.

Bibliographical Note

Sea Life Mandalas Coloring Book is a new work,
first published by Dover Publications, Inc., in 2017.

International Standard Book Number

ISBN-13: 978-0-486-81378-3
ISBN-10: 0-486-81378-9

Manufactured in the United States by LSC Communications
81378901   2017
www.doverpublications.com

Flying fish

Rock lobsters